GEO. NEWNES L^TD. Southampton Street & Exeter Street Strand.

LADIES!

A brighter picture than a young lady in frosty weather, with her sprightly step and rosy cheeks and flashing eyes, it is impossible to conceive. It implies comfortable clothing, suitable nourishment, and sufficient exercise. Sluggish digestion or insufficient nutriment would spoil all. The blood must be kept coursing briskly through the veins. A little BOVRIL will agree with the most delicate organism, and will make the eye sparkle and the cheek tingle; whilst tea or coffee, delightful as we confess them to be, would blanch the complexion and disturb the nerves.

A young gentleman, trying to explain the secret of success in love matters, broke into verse: we forbear quoting in full, but the refrain was—

"BOVRIL DID IT!"

As we cannot expect ladies to be equally communicative on such themes, never till the end of time, mayhap, will it be known how much BOVRIL has aided them in their conquests and completed their triumphs.

I

WORKS BY JOHN RUSKIN.

Examples of the Architecture of Venice. Selected and Drawn to Measurement from the Edifices. With the Text and the Sixteen Plates as originally published. The Plates and Text (unbound), in cloth cover, on atlas folio (about 25 inches by 17½ inches), price £3 3s.

The Stones of Venice. A New and Complete Edition (imperial 8vo) in 3 Vols. With the 53 Plates and all the Woodcuts and Text as originally issued. £4 9s. Cloth.

A History of the rise, prosperity, and decline of Venice, as manifested in the architecture of the City.

The Stones of Venice. Selections for Use of Travellers in Venice and Verona. In 2 vols., small post 8vo, cloth, 5s. each. Fourth Edition.

St. Mark's Rest. The History of Venice. Written for the help of the few Travellers who still care for her Monuments. 12mo, complete in cloth, 6s.

Guide to Pictures in the Academy of Fine Arts, Venice. New complete Edition, revised and corrected. In one part, 1s., 8vo.

Mornings in Florence. Being Simple Studies of Christian Art for English Travellers. Third Edition, cloth, 4s.

Roadside Songs of Tuscany. Translated and Illustrated by FRANCESCA ALEXANDER, and Edited by JOHN RUSKIN. With articles by Mr. Ruskin on Domestic Usefulness, the Virtues necessary to Sainthood, the Priest's Office and Gipsy Character, &c.; also Preface and Editorial Notes.

In Ten Parts, each containing Two Illustrations by the Platinotype Process, from Drawings by Miss Alexander 7s., each Part; or the Complete Work, in cloth, £3 10s., medium 4to.

GEORGE ALLEN, Orpington; and 8, Bell Yard, Temple Bar, London.

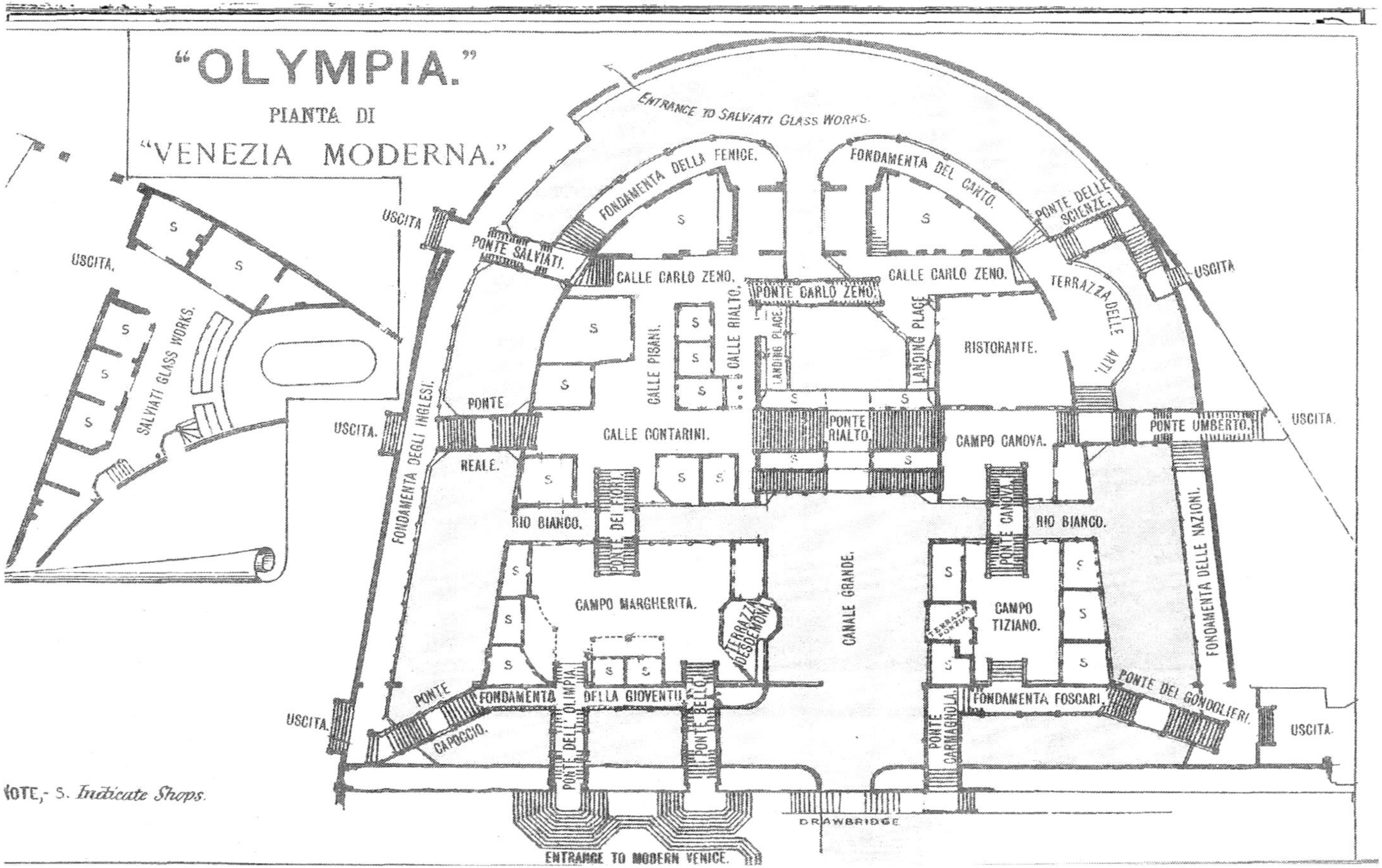
"OLYMPIA."
PIANTA DI
"VENEZIA MODERNA."
ENTRANCE TO SALVIATI GLASS WORKS.
SALVIATI GLASS WORKS.
USCITA.
FONDAMENTA DELLA FENICE.
FONDAMENTA DEL CANTO.
PONTE DELLE SCIENZE.
PONTE SALVIATI.
CALLE CARLO ZENO.
PONTE CARLO ZENO.
TERRAZZA DELLE ARTI.
RISTORANTE.
CALLE PISANI.
CALLE RIALTO.
LANDING PLACE.
FONDAMENTA DEGLI INGLESI.
PONTE
REALE.
CALLE CONTARINI.
PONTE RIALTO.
CAMPO CANOVA.
PONTE UMBERTO.
RIO BIANCO.
PONTE DEI FIORI.
PONTE CANOVA.
FONDAMENTA DELLE NAZIONI.
CAMPO MARGHERITA.
TERRAZZA DESDEMONA.
CANALE GRANDE.
CAMPO TIZIANO.
TERRAZZA PORZIA.
PONTE CAPOCCIO.
FONDAMENTA DELLA GIOVENTU.
PONTE DELL' OLIMPIA.
PONTE BELLO.
PONTE CARMAGNOLA.
FONDAMENTA FOSCARI.
PONTE DEI GONDOLIERI.
DRAWBRIDGE
ENTRANCE TO MODERN VENICE.
NOTE,- S. Indicate Shops.
S

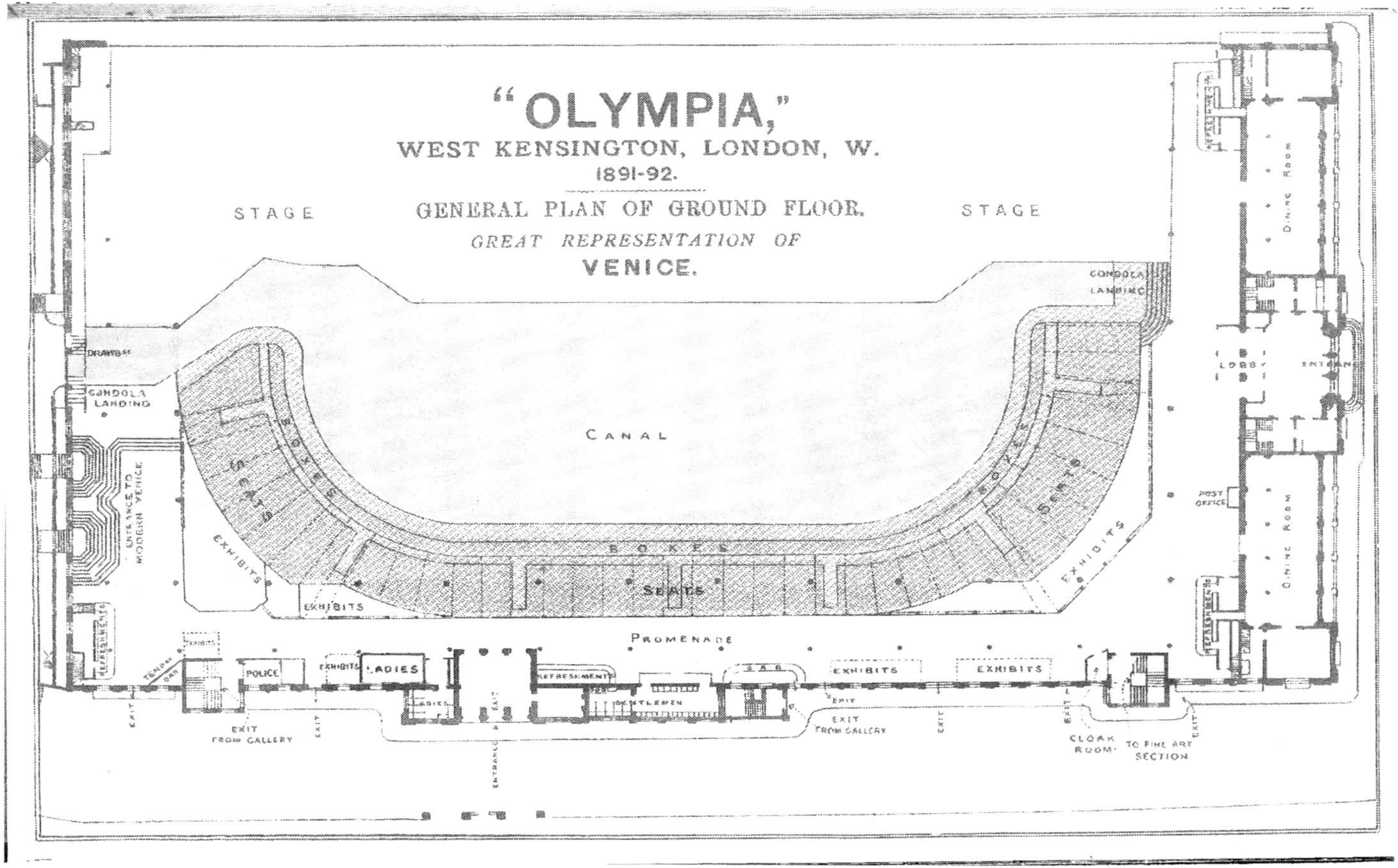
"OLYMPIA,"
WEST KENSINGTON, LONDON, W.
1891-92.
GENERAL PLAN OF GROUND FLOOR.
GREAT REPRESENTATION OF
VENICE.
STAGE
STAGE
CANAL
BOXES
BOXES
BOXES
SEATS
SEATS
SEATS
GONDOLA LANDING
GONDOLA LANDING
ENTRANCE TO MODERN VENICE
EXHIBITS
EXHIBITS
EXHIBITS
EXHIBITS
EXHIBITS
EXHIBITS
PROMENADE
POLICE
LADIES
REFRESHMENTS
GENTLEMEN
EXIT
EXIT FROM GALLERY
ENTRANCE & EXIT
CLOAK ROOM
TO FINE ART SECTION
LOBBY
POST OFFICE
DINING ROOM
DINING ROOM

VENICE:

THE BRIDE OF THE SEA.

A GRAND

HISTORIC AND ROMANTIC SPECTACLE AND

AQUATIC PAGEANT.

BY

IMRE KIRALFY,

Author and Producer of

NERO, COLUMBUS, BABYLON, ETC., ETC.

PUBLISHED BY GEORGE NEWNES, LIMITED,
SOUTHAMPTON STREET AND EXETER STREET, STRAND,
LONDON, W.C.

NOTICE TO ADVERTISERS.

All communications respecting ADVERTISING MATTERS of any kind in connection with "Venice at Olympia" must be addressed to

MR. JOHN HART,

Advertising Agent and Contractor,

17 & 18, ARUNDEL STREET,

STRAND, LONDON. W.C.

IMRE KIRALFY.

ALL
who suffer from,
INDIGESTION.
General Debility.
LOSS OF APPETITE.
Dyspepsia.
LIVER COMPLAINT.
Nervous Headaches.
BILIOUSNESS.
Costiveness.
Should use Camomile in its most convenient form.
VIZ
NORTON'S · CAMOMILE · PILLS
REGISTERED.
TRADE NORTON'S MARK.
Sold everywhere, price 13½d., 2s. 9d. & 11s.

INTRODUCTORY.

IN my childhood's days Venice was well known to me from frequent residences there, and the spell that the erstwhile Queen of the Adriatic cast over me has never been charmed away by contact with more modern or pretentious cities.

The general surroundings, the silence of the streets of water, the exquisite tone of the noble buildings, so dear to the artistic eye, the historic and legendary associations, the very movements and liquid accents of the inhabitants had, and still have, an indescribable charm for me. So strong was the glamour, that it has always been my ambition to present to the public a spectacle which should have for its foundation some stirring incident in the remarkable history of what was once the centre of European commerce and civilization, combined with a realistic reproduction, on a somewhat reduced scale, of the City itself.

In all my travels and sojournings throughout the world, I never, until I saw Olympia, beheld an edifice that I could deem suitable for the production of such a spectacle; and my association with Olympia, in connection with my production of "Nero" there in 1889, convinced me that at last I had found a structure that would answer all my requirements.

It was not, however, until July last that I seriously turned my attention to what I had long determined should be my *chef d'œuvre.* To think was to act, and within the short space of six months the stupendous work has been created, elaborated, and perfected.

Many and frequent visits of late to Venice have still more impressed on my mind the beauties which now remain of her ancient grandeur, and these I have endeavoured faithfully to reproduce in our "MODERN VENICE AT OLYMPIA." Here is an exact copy—true to scale, a fac-simile in colouring—of Venice of to-day; her bridges, buildings, streets and canals are accurately copied, even to the fact of her watery highways having Venetian gondolas floating on them, steered and propelled by expert native gondoliers, who here ply their vocation in the same manner as they have been accustomed to do on the palace-lined canals of their home.

It would seem bombastic were I here to recount all the enormous difficulties that had to be overcome, in order to bring within one covered edifice so vast an undertaking, for it has been practically the building of a city; not an ideal city, but a city that is now replete with life and activity, a city of the living, not of the dead.

As usual, before commencing the construction of

one of my historic spectacles, I made myself thoroughly acquainted with the history of the country with which I proposed to deal, and in the pursuit of my studies I found that the epoch of the Chioggian wars was not only most suitable for the purpose of spectacular production, but that it contained exceptionally strong situations. This period was one of the most remarkable and interesting in the history of Venice, for she then passed through her greatest crisis, and emerged from these wars weakened and crippled in forces, it is true, but covered with glory arising from some of her most famous naval and military victories.

The period of 1378 to 1380 was truly a remarkable one. Beset by powerful foes, Venice seemed doomed, but the spirit of patriotism was strong, and when an appeal was made to the citizens for men to fight for the preservation of their city, it was found that every man who was capable of bearing arms had subscribed his name as being willing and ready to fight for his country. Nay, more than that, when it was found that the public treasury needed replenishing, being depleted by protracted campaigns, the women of every class brought their last jewels to the public coffers.

Still more noticeable was this period on account of the three great heroes who lived contemporaneously, namely the Doge, Andrea Contarini, who, at the advanced age of 72, fired by the wonderful result of his appeal to the citizens, in person led them to battle and victory; Vettore Pisani, one of the bravest and most successful Admirals Venice ever boasted of, and Carlo Zeno, their brave and renowned General.

Having decided to select this period as the date of my historic spectacle, my next care was to find some romantic story which could be advantageously interwoven with the historic truths. Where could I better turn than to the pages of the greatest poet the world has ever produced—England's immortal Shakespeare. And what story so fitting as the one so exquisitely told in his sublime play of the "The Merchant of Venice."

But before I could positively decide that I might consistently combine this beautiful romance with the stern facts of history, I made a careful collation of all the authorities on Shakespeare, as well as a study of the sources from whence he drew the story. To my intense delight I found that not only was there not anything incongruous, but that everything tended to make my selection as happy as I could possibly desire.

Having thus the materials for my story ready, I set to work to elaborate and construct the spectacle with an earnest enthusiasm; an enthusiasm such as never fired me in any of my previous labours, and I leave it to a discerning and appreciative British public to judge my work, and trust that it will be as well received as was my first production in England—"Nero."

IMRE KIRALFY.

LONDON, *7th December*, 1891.

DRAMATIS PERSONÆ.

ANDREA CONTARINI	*Doge of Venice.*
VETTORE PISANI	*Admiral of the Fleet.*
CARLO ZENO	*Captain-General.*
MICHEALO STENO	*A Venetian Noble.*
TADDEO GIUSINIANI	*Captain-General.*
PIETRO MOCENIGO	*Secretary io the Doge.*
GASPARO SPINOLA	*A Genoese General.*
ANTONIO	*A Venetian Merchant.*
BASSANIO, LORENZO, GRATIANO	*His Friends.*
MARINO CORBANO	*An old Seaman and Patriot.*
MATTEO FASEOLO	*A Townsman of Chioggia.*
GIUSEPPÉ AND GIOVANNI	*His Sons.*
SHYLOCK	*A Money Lender.*
TUBAL	*His Friend.*
A Notary.	*A Gaoler.*
VALENTINA VISCONTI	*Bride of Pietro II. of Cyprus.*
PORTIA	*A Wealthy Heiress.*
NERISSA	*Companion to Portia.*
JESSICA	*Shylock's Daughter.*
BIANCA	*Corbano's Daughter.*

Venetian, Genoese, Paduan, Dalmatian, and Greek Soldiers, and Mercenaries. Nobles, Citizens, Pages, Artizans and Labourers, etc., etc., etc

The following EMINENT MASTERS of their respective arts have assisted in the Spectacular Production of this

MASTERLY CREATION OF

IMRE KIRALFY,

ENTITLED

VENICE:

The Bride of the Sea.

THE MUSIC SPECIALLY COMPOSED BY

Signor ANGELO VENANZI.

Composer of the Charming Music of Imre Kiralfy's Nero, Columbus, etc.

THE ITALIAN POETRY AND WORDS OF SONGS BY

Signor ANGELO BIGNOTTI.

COSTUMES AND ACCESSORIES SPECIALLY DESIGNED BY

WILHELM,

To whom the Author is indebted for some valuable suggestions.

THE SCENERY DESIGNED AND PAINTED BY

MM. AMABLE & GARDY.

STAGE AND CHORÉOGRAPHIC DIRECTOR

Signor ETTORE COPPINI.

MUSICAL LEADER AND VOCAL CONDUCTOR

Sig. B. LOMBARDI.

STAGE MECHANISM AND GENERAL ILLUMINATIONS UNDER THE DIRECTION OF

Mr. W. A. BOND.

THE STRUCTURES IN MODERN VENICE ERECTED BY THE FOLLOWING FIRMS:

THE PLASTIC DECORATION CO., Messrs. J. & R. BROWN, Mons. ALBINET, Signor CASANOVA, and Signor ALBERTI.

THE INTERIOR DECORATIONS OF THE CAFÉ RIALTO AND ROYAL BOX BY THE

LIGNOMUR CO.

THE ARCHITECTURAL WORK UNDER THE DIRECTION OF

Mr. WILSON BENNISON.

THE MALE COSTUMES AND ACCESSORIES BY

Mons. EDMOND LANDOLFF.

THE LADIES' COSTUMES EXECUTED BY

Miss FISHER.

THE COSTUMES OF THE CARNIVAL BALLET AND AQUATIC PAGEANT OF THE SEASONS BY

Mons. ALIAS.

THE COSTUMES OF THE RAINBOW EFFECT BY

Messrs. J. SIMMONS & SON.

CARTONAGE, STATUARY AND SCULPTURE OF THE ENTIRE SPECTACLE BY

Mons. CHARLES HALLÉ.

THE VENETIAN ILLUMINATING EFFECTS AND GRAND FINALE BY

RANCATI & CO.

THE WIGS BY

CLARKSON.

THE STAINED GLASS BY

Mr. EDWARD FRAMPTON.

THE PEAL OF BELLS BY

Messrs. HARRINGTON, LATHOM & CO.

THIS ENTIRE GIGANTIC PRODUCTION, CONCEIVED, CREATED AND DESIGNED BY

IMRE KIRALFY,

AND PRODUCED UNDER HIS PERSONAL DIRECTION AND SUPERVISION.

IMRE KIRALFY, LIMITED,

COMMITTEE OF MANAGEMENT:—

JOSEPH LYONS, ESQ. *(Chairman)*

JOHN HART, ESQ. MONTAGUE GLUCKSTEIN, ESQ.

HAROLD HARTLEY, ESQ.

Secretary and Treasurer.—HERMAN HART ESQ.

GENERAL SYNOPSIS OF SCENES & INCIDENTS OF THE GREAT SPECTACLE.

ACT I. SCENE I.

A Public Place before the Arsenal of Venice, A.D., 1378.

Grand Chorus of Artizans.
Victorious Procession.
Return of Pisani.
Ceremony of the Launch of "The Adriatica."
Valentina's Imposing Departure from Venezia la Bella.

Mimic Battle upon the Arsenal Bridge.

SCENE II.

Portia's Palatial Home.

Terpsichorean Revels.
Reception of the Suitors.
The Ordeal of the Caskets.
The Triumph of Love.
The Departure for Venice.

SCENE III.

Grand View of the Piazzetta San Marco.

Approaching Trial of the Merchant.
Bianca, the Mad Girl.
Result of the Trial.

GRAND AQUATIC CARNIVAL BALLET

INVENTED, DESIGNED, AND PRODUCED BY

IMRE KIRALFY.

1. **ENTRANCE OF MASKERS** *by the Grande Corps de Ballet.*
2. **DANCE OF MUSICAL BELLS** *by the* 32 *Secondes danseuses.*
3. **GREAT XYLOPHONE DANCE** *by* 32 *Ballineré distincte.*
4. **SUPERB MARINE BALABILETTO** *by* 350 *danseuses.*

Peal of Alarm from the Bells of the Campanile.

News of the Fall of Chioggia.
The deliverance of Admiral Pisani from Prison.
Doge Contarini's Promise to Lead the Venetians to Victory.
Blessing the Banner of St. Mark.
Departure for the Final Struggle.

INTERVAL OF FIFTEEN MINUTES.

ACT II. SCENE I.

The Fortress of Chioggia.

The Genoese Bivouac.
Military Dances.
Approach of the Venetian Fleet.
View of a Naval encounter and Genoese Victory.
General Rejoicing and Military Fete.
The Approach of Zeno's Fleet.
The Last Defence of the Genoese.

STORMING OF CHIOGGIA AND TRIUMPH OF THE VENETIANS.

SCENE II.

The Island of Lido.

Aquatic Games, Sports and Tournaments.
MAJESTIC AQUATIC PAGEANT
And Return of the Victors.
Impressive Ceremony of the Marriage of the Adriatic.
Ancient Venetian Regatta.
Realistic Gondola Races.

SCENE III.

Terrace near Portia's Palace.

THE GRANDEST SCENIC REPRESENTATION EVER PRESENTED.
Grand Banquet given to the Conquerors.
Departure of the Liberated Genoese Captives.
Enchanting Ballet of the Triumph of Love.
Bewitching Divertissement—Morning, Noon, Evening, Night.

TERMINATING WITH A MOST GORGEOUS

ILLUMINATED AL FRESCO FÊTE.

ARGUMENT.

ACT I.

Scene I.

THE ARSENAL OF VENICE.

A.D 1378.

THE opening displays an animated scene in the Venetian Arsenal, where the numerous work-people, who have been employed in building "The Adriatica," are making great preparations for a national holiday on the completion of their work. The final touches are being given to the vessel, and each department is using every endeavour to be the first to complete its share of the work.

Male Chorus.

Come, haste, our task is nearly done,
And all the work now joins in one.
Strike, strike upon the iron glowing,
Swift through our veins new life is flowing.

Uomini.

Su presto; l'opra—è omai finita;
Cessano l'ansie—cessa il lavor.
Su batti; batti—che il ferro incita
Con nova vita—novo valor.

Female Chorus.

When tossed by waves, when wild winds howl;
When pirates round, like sea-wolves, prowl;
Sail on, proud bark, all dangers scorn.
Sail on, through night to breezy morn.

Donne.

In mezzo all'onda,—in mezzo al mare
Di sponda in sponda—di cielo in ciel,
Da mane a sera—dovrai vogare
Placida, altera—nave fedel.

United Chorus.

Strike! 'neath your blows the anvils ring.
Steady! keep time with measured swing.
Our songs of joy will reach the sky,
And "Venice Free" shall be our cry.

Tutti.

Su batti; all'opra—presto il lavoro
Gagliardo e fiero—dovrà finir;
E s'alzi all'etra—di festa un coro;
Venezia libera—potrà—gioir.

A general rejoicing takes place, the ship being nearly ready for the launch. Bassanio, Lorenzo, and Gratiano enter and meet their friend Antonio. Antonio is ill at ease, having all his fortune embarked on the sea; and has just received bad news concerning one of his ships.

Bassanio confesses that he has impoverished himself, and that he owes much to Antonio; and, acknowledging his love for Portia, a wealthy lady of Belmont, asks Antonio to once more assist him, so that he may present himself in a fitting manner to equal the other suitors for Portia's hand.

Antonio, rich merchant as he is, again explains that he has all his fortunes embarked at sea, and cannot himself provide the money his friend needs, but that his credit is at his friend's disposal.

Shylock, a money-lender of Venice, passing, is applied to by Bassanio for the loan of three thousand ducats, for the repayment of which Antonio is willing

to be surety. After some apparent hesitation, Shylock agrees to lend the money required, but, to the surprise of all, offers it without interest.

The proposal, however, has a condition, which is that Antonio, as surety, shall, "in a merry sport," sign a bond, stipulating that a pound of his flesh shall be cut off by Shylock if the money be not paid within the time agreed upon.

Bassanio declares that he would rather dwell in his necessity than his friend should seal such a bond for him, and place his life in such jeopardy. But Antonio, confident of his ability to repay the money within the time, over-rules his objections.

A Notary is summoned to prepare the bond, the requisite instructions are given him, and the party then proceed to his office to sign the document. Shylock, in high glee, for his proposal to lend the money without interest is but a scheme to get Antonio into his power, rubs his hands, and congratulates himself on the opportunity he has of feeding the ancient grudge he bears Antonio.

While these negotiations are in progress, Jessica, Shylock's daughter, is seen handing a letter to her father's servant, to be delivered by him to Lorenzo, who is in love with her. She returns his passion, and in this letter is agreeing to elope with him. She re-enters the house, and from a window sees the servant call Lorenzo aside, just as he is going with Antonio and the others to the Notary's, and gives him the letter. Lorenzo reads it and is delighted, and, following his friends, throws kisses to Jessica at her window.

The action now changes, and the Venetian Admiral, Pisano, who has just achieved a great sea-victory over the Genoese Admiral, Luigi Fieschi, in which he captured five vessels and a large number of prisoners, including Fieschi himself, and the flower of the Genoese nobility, returns to Venice, and a

GRAND TRIUMPHAL PROCESSION

appears.

The work-people, excited and flushed with the victory, rush tumultuously to see the pageant, and the populace accord a welcome to the conquering heroes worthy of the deeds done.

The work on the Ship being now completed, the consummation of all the toil is attained by the

"LAUNCH OF ADRIATICA,"

which takes place amidst general rejoicings. This Launch is looked upon as a great event, for it is confidently anticipated that the supremacy of Venice will be well and worthily sustained by this important addition to their already powerful fleet. The assembled citizens unite in a

Stirring Chorus,

Proud vessel, glide unto the sea,
And safely ride the dashing foam.
Far, far to other shores may she
In all her strength and beauty roam.

The helmsman sings a song of pride
To greet thee, challenge thrown to fate.
Dolphins shall play around thy side,
Sea nymphs thy victories relate.

Scendi in mar e via per l'onda
Voga, voga ad altri lidi;
Lieta a flutti va e confidi
La tua forza e il tuo poter.

Scendi in mar, sfida gioconda
Gitta ai torbidi destini;
Va, fra najadi e delfini
Sposa canto abil nocchier.

Noble bark, thou art our glory !
To Venice thou wilt honour bring
Distant nations hear the story,
How of "Venice free" we sing.

Noble bark, bear forth our standard
Flutt'ring proudly in the breeze.
Venice, by her fleet defended,
Rules supreme on all the seas.

Salve, della repubblica
Vanto ed onor sei tu.
Canta ai lontani popoli
Dell' Adria le virtù.

Or di Venezia libera
Narra qual sia il valor.
Voga ; della repubblica
Gloria sei tu ed onor.

THE ADIEU OF VALENTINA TO VENICE

is made in the midst of the nobility and wealth of the City. Valentina, the lovely daughter of the proud Visconti, is embarking to meet with her royal betrothed, Peter II., of Cyprus.

The departure is signalised with marked honors by the Venetian Government, and Valentina is escorted to her royal and luxurious state barge by Admiral Pisani himself, and representatives of the leading noble families of Venice. Special guards and a brilliant retinue of gaily clad pages accompany the bride elect to her new home.

A tearful leave-taking casts a slight gloom over the brilliant party, but under sunny skies, and in such a gay scene, tears soon give place to happy looks, and amidst the good wishes and congratulations of her friends, Valentina bids farewell to her native city.

Shylock now appears at the threshold of his house and gives Jessica his keys, as he is going out, and knowing that the night will be devoted to festivities, he strictly enjoins her not to show herself at the windows, or to leave the house, after which he departs.

Lorenzo, accompanied by a few friends, approaches Shylock's house. He calls, and Jessica appears at a window, and after handing him a casket of Jewels goes off with Lorenzo and his friends in the Gondola to be married.

Darkness has long since fallen, but the closing of the people's gaieties and revels culminates in a night's festive sports.

Two rival factions, Castelani and Nocolotti, are represented by volunteers, and they engage in a

Mimic Battle on the Arsenal Bridge,

in the course of which, many of the contestants are hurled from the bridge into the water below. The object in this mock combat being to effect a crossing of the bridge over the prostrate bodies of opponents.

The vanquished party, annoyed at their defeat, recommence hostilities, but not in the same spirit, and the Mimic Battle speedily turns into a real, and very fierce one, which is only ended by the Military Authorities separating the now enraged contestants.

Whilst all this has been going on Shylock returns, and finds that his daughter has fled, taking with her a very considerable portion of his wealth. He frantically seizes a torch, and, half maddened at the loss of his wealth and his daughter, forces his way into the midst of the revellers. At the same time a festive party, returning from a Banquet, join the crowd, and continue their festivities with the populace.

SCENE II.

PALATIAL HOME OF PORTIA.

The friends and attendants of the lovely Portia, amongst whom are the newly married Lorenzo and Jessica, assemble at her Villa at Belmont, where the magnificence of the surroundings rival the brilliancy of a regal Court. Her beauty, goodness and virtues are extolled in a

MAIDEN'S CHORUS.

Fair maiden, pure and mild—with love thou hast beguiled,	O mesta vergine— bella e gentile
All those who scan thy face—thou dame of noble race.	Come una rosa— nata in aprile ;
As fair as rose new born—just bursting forth at morn.	Dagli occhi belli— piove l'incanto
Thy virtues are a charm—to shield thee from all harm.	Placido e santo— d'un casto amor.
Soon wilt thou feel love's dart—implanted in thy heart.	Le tue virtudi— la tua dolcezza
But healed with lover's kiss—thou'lt prove all earthly bliss.	Come carezza— scende a ogni cor.

With a brilliant escort, the swarthy Prince of Morocco comes to swell the already large number of those who have been attracted to Belmont by the fame of Portia's beauty and wealth. The charms of the fair hostess have evidently not been exaggerated to him, and he is captivated by his reception.

Quickly following him comes the Prince of Arragon, a proud Spaniard, who arrives with an imposing retinue, befitting his high rank.

Dazzled by the pomp and splendour around him as well as by the graces of Portia, he, like all the others, is a willing victim to love.

Last among the arrivals is Bassanio, who, enriched with the ducats lent by Shylock, under Antonio's bond, comes in a style worthy of the occasion. Portia and Bassanio had met before, and the favourable impression he had then made upon her heart had been a lasting one, as is evinced by the warmth of his reception.

To entertain her guests Portia has made arrangements for a dance, and at a signal given by her all the maidens present join in

TERPSICHORE'S REVELS.

The dance ended, Portia relates the story of her father's will, by which she is debarred from making her own selection of a husband. She must marry the suitor who is fortunate enough to select the casket which contains her portrait, there being three caskets, one each of gold, silver, and lead. The terms upon which selection is made are hard, compelling the suitor who selects the wrong one to depart instantly, never to divulge the secret of the casket he had chosen; and "Never to speak to lady afterward in way of marriage."

When all the suitors for the hand of their beautiful entertainer had assented to these conditions, and while the air resounds with the melodies of his native land, sung by sweet-voiced girls, the Prince of Morocco, hopeful and courageous, proceeds to make his selection of one of the caskets which shall bring him joy, or despair.

All that glitters may not be gold,
So says a proverb, 'tis true though d.
This proverb truly may have a charm,
Oh, Prince, beware, beware,
To shield thee from ll, to save from harm.
Oh, Prince, take care.

Quel ch' è lucente—non è tutt'or,
Proverbio è questo—in uso ancor
Proverbio strano—che a un talismano
Virtude ha ugual.
Oh! Guarda! Principe; ti adesca il vano
Baglior del mal.

Hidden from the gaze of the other suitors he chooses the casket of gold, and then pauses for an instant to summon his resolution to calmly abide the result. He unlocks the casket, raises its lid and is horror-stricken at the contents. He sees that he was unfortunate in his choice, and bows his respectful adieu to Portia as he retires from her presence.

The Prince of Arragon, the flower of Spanish chivalry, is the next to take the step which shall bring to his heart happiness or misery, and the gentle maidens seek to inspire him by singing the melodies of his own romantic land.

Behold! who comes his fate to learn
Of Spain, the hope and pride.
'Twixt love and war in that fair land
Swiftly the days do glide.

The Andalusian beauties dark
On thee their smiles do bend;
May fortune good thy portion be,
And joy thy steps attend.

Ecco il principe cortese
D'Aragona giunto, or, or . . .
É la Spagna il bel paese
Della guerra e dell'amor.

L'Andalusa ardita e bruna
Ti sorride, o giovin Sir . . .
T' accompagna la fortuna
Coll' ardente tuo desir.

During this song he makes his choice and opens the casket of silver to find in it only disappointment for his fondest dreams. He sadly bids farewell to all, and retires with his impressive escort.

Now comes the poor, brave, and hopeful Venetian youth, Bassanio, who has long adored the lovely Portia. With trepidation he approaches the recess which hides the caskets from view. He pauses, and then raising the cover of the leaden receptacle of his future fate for joy or sorrow, a vision of ecstacy meets his gaze in the picture of her in whom all his blissful hopes are centred. His most extravagant dream of happiness is to be realized, and overcome by his emotions he kneels before the portrait of his idol in a whirl of bewildering delight.

We see every hour—love's wonderful power, None can escape his dart. Of young and of old—the story is told, Love's arrows pierce the heart. Both humble and great all share the same fate.	Salve d'amore—bel vincitore; Tu vittorioso alter Volle il destin—forte, divin Che il gaudio ed il mister Ti scendessero in core—bel vincitore.

Portia now greets him with effusion and he claims her as his bride.

Gratiano and Nerissa request to have their affections sealed in matrimony. Gratiano explains that Nerissa had promised to be his bride if Bassanio is successful in his choice. Portia joyfully assents, and Gratiano also expresses his approval.

Portia and Nerissa each place on their lover's finger a ring, and extract the promise that the ring will never be parted with while life remains.

This scene of joy is interrupted by the sudden arrival of a gondola which brings a hurried messenger from Antonio with tidings of his perilous position. His ships have been delayed at sea and, he is, consequently, unable to meet his obligations to Shylock, who now demands his bond. While Bassanio is reading this intelligence, Portia, his fair intended, perceives his agitation, and on her entreaty, he hands the letter to her. Portia on reading it urges his instant departure, no time is to be lost, the friend must be rescued; and bidding his love a hasty farewell, himself and companions depart to plan the rescue of Antonio.

Portia now places Jessica and Lorenzo in charge of her household, while she orders her barge to be prepared for a journey. Meanwhile, Nerissa brings some legal robes for their disguise. Portia is already aboard her barge anxiously awaiting her return, which is followed by their immediate departure for Venice.

SCENE III.

Attention is now directed to the

GRAND CANAL, AND
THE PIAZZETTA SAN MARCO.

A throng of people are hovering between anxiety and expectation caused by the

APPROACHING TRIAL OF THE MERCHANT.

Contarini, the aged and noble

DOGE OF VENICE,

now appears in state cortege, preceded by

THE PATRIARCH, THE NOBILITY & DIGNITARIES,

and followed by the Ambassadors, the Council of Three, the Council of Ten, etc., etc., and proceeds to the Ducal Palace to preside at the legal proceedings.

A gaoler brings in Antonio followed by his dear friends Bassanio and Gratiano, while Shylock is seen crossing the bridge leading to San Marco.

The populace, filled with anger against the holder of the bond, endeavour to force their way into the Hall of Justice, but are prevented by the Ducal Guard.

A barge now approaches, and from it disembarks the fair Portia robed as a doctor of laws, and Nerissa clad as her clerk. The latter disappears for a moment into the Ducal Palace to deliver a letter, but soon returns, and both then hurry into the Palace.

Bianca, the beautiful daughter of Corbano, has suddenly become demented on account of the news she has received that her betrothed has been captured, and probably killed, in a meleé with the Genoese. The poor girl rushes upon the Piazza and is followed by the populace, who are surprised and filled with sympathy to see their favourite in such distress. Her father, Marino Corbano, passing by chance, recognises his daughter with the most poignant grief, for she does not appear to know him. Gazing on the mass of people who have gathered round her, she at length recognises her bosom friend Coralia, and for a few moments her reason returns. Half choked with tears and sobs she tells those present that her lover, Carlo Cavaro, who had joined the army of the Republic, has been captured by the enemy, and that probably by this time death has been his doom.

Bianca makes an heroic vow to disguise herself in male attire, join the soldiery at the first opportunity, and either find her lover or avenge his death. Prostrate and overcome by the mental strain, the beautiful Bianca is led away by her father and her friends to her parental home.

Shouts of joy are now heard within the palace and Antonio's victory is assured. Shylock, defeated, pale, haggard, and almost frantic with despair, emerges from the trial, and is only rescued from the fury of the mob by the interference of the Ducal Guards, when his intended victim and friends are seen, and the wrath of the throng is replaced by shouts of applause.

The young and brilliantly successful lawyer and his clerk now appear, are boisterously congratulated, and offered great pecuniary rewards, but the youthful advocate will only accept as momentoes, the much prized rings worn by Bassanio and Gratiano.

This request is strenuously objected to by Bassanio, but when urged by Antonio, they yield, with heavy forebodings, and regretfully surrender the rings. The lawyer and his assistant hastily leave, going in the direction taken by the unhappy money-lender. This happy finale to what might have been a wicked tragedy is signalized by general rejoicing which culminates with

A Marvellous Marine Ballet

TOGETHER WITH

ECCENTRIC DANCES AND MUSICAL GEMS,

INVENTED BY

MR. IMRE KIRALFY.

THE GREAT BELL OF THE CAMPANILE NOW TOLLS NOTES OF ALARM,

the dancers fly in terror, while armed and partially

armed citizens dash on in wild confusion owing to the arrival of a courier with the depressing news of the

FALL OF CHIOGGIA.

The consternation caused by this announcement could not have been exceeded if Venice herself had been captured.

Terrified women rush frightened through the streets, expressing their grief by shrill cries and vehement gesticulations of despair. The men whom the alarm bell had called to arms are, for the most part, silent and dejected, but a large number are fired with a burning desire to defend their homes and families even with their lives.

Doge Contarini also responds to his country's needs, and summons his Council to consider and act at once, so as to alleviate the desperate situation.

Merchants, burghers, marines, artizans, and soldiers now eagerly crowd to the palace gates, inspired by the noble impulse of patriotism, and demand the immediate release of their admiral and idol, Vettore Pisani. This is emphasized by the voices of the men in

AN EFFECTIVE VOCAL DEMONSTRATION.

Soon our hero, our great leader, Must be free from prison's chain. We demand it, and the people, Like the gods, ne'er ask in vain.	Il grand' eroe,—il nostro capitan Sia tosto in libertá Iddio lo vuol; e il popolo, no, in van Chiesto giammai non ha.

Pietro Mocenigo now brings the welcome tidings that the Senate has conceded the popular demand, which is further confirmed by the appearance of Michel Steno.

Yes, in answer to our cry,
Our great chief again is free.
Without him our hopes would die.
Now we'll fight for liberty.
Doge and Senate have agreed
Our great leader must be freed.

Long live the Doge,
Hurrah ! hurrah !

Now all our troubles soon will be done,
Brightly to cheer us shineth the sun.
Chains fall asunder, doors open fly,
Rulers must bow low, when people cry.

Del popolo al voler
Che brama il gran guerrier
Libero ancor . . .
Il Doge ed il Senato
Hanno la libertà tosto accordato
Pel suo valor—al grande condottier.

(*Popolo* 1 *parte*).—Viva il Doge.
2 „ —Evviva, evviva.

Tutti.

Oh alfin cessino le pene
Splenda il sol libero in ciel;
Siano sciolte le catene
Al campion forte e fedel.

The people then flock to the prison to bear to Pisani the news of his freedom.

In the meantime the Doge's ambassadors, with seven noble prisoners, who are to be unconditionally restored to the enemy, depart for the Genoese Camp, with the view of securing peace at any price.

After Mocenigo and Steno have passed the prison gates, Pisani is seen behind the bars endeavouring to pacify the populace, but the enthusiasm becomes so great that all barriers are passed and

PISANI IS BORNE IN TRIUMPH TO THE PALACE

on the shoulders of the patriotic sailors, and the multitude join in a joyous martial refrain,

Hurrah ! hurrah ! with vict'ry crowned
The rhythm of our song shall rise
Like golden music to the skies.
Our fav'rite is no longer bound.
Hurrah ! hurrah ! hurrah !

Vittoria, vittoria,
S'innalzi per l'etra
Il suon di aurea cetra
Coll'inno di gloria
Vittoria, vittoria. . . .

The Doge's Secretary calls upon the citizens for volunteers.

Come, citizens, defend your land,
Danger is threatened all around.
Our foemen press on every hand,
To silken fetters be not bound.
Let each man strive to be the first
To answer this, my call to arms.
A coward is a thing accursed,
Brave men rejoice in war's alarms.

Cittadini la patria è in periglio
Forti in armi accorete a pugnar,
La miseria ci opprime; e ogni figlio
Corra ardito la patria a salvar.
Su presto, ò cittadini,
Ch'io non vimplori invan;
Pei vecchi e pei bambini
Offrite obolo e pan.

Pietro Mocenigo, standing upon an elevated dais, is seen receiving the signatures of those who are willing to volunteer to fight for the defence of their country, and he soon exhibits the lists. The throng is very great, every man in Venice having affixed his signature to that document. The women in great masses are also on hand to contribute to the general safety by donating their money, jewels, and other valuables for the public weal. Portia and Nerissa veiled, followed by a numerous retinue, bring treasures of great value to the Government representatives. They recognize their lovers among the volunteering patriots, and are deeply impressed by their self-sacrifice.

The Doge Contarini now arrives, and being shown the great donations and the list of subscribers to the National War Fund resolves to take part in the conflict by leading the fleet into action against his country's foes.

He recognizes Bassanio and Gratiano, and compliments them upon their devotion to their flag; but when he sees Portia surrounded by her maids of honor, and notes the wealth she has bestowed upon the national cause, he blesses her and kisses her hand in token of his great esteem. Then

THE OLD FLAGS OF SAN MARCO ARE UNFURLED

and the Doge reminds his people that under these same

banners the Venetians had brought defeat and discomfiture to the powerful Barbarossa.

At this instant ambassadors in quest of peace return from their mission to Doria, and proclaim that they have failed. Amid excited plaudits, the Doge enters San Marco, followed by his supporters, and receives a blessing prior to his departure for the scene of battle.

The booming of cannons is now heard in the distance, and all the warriors present, inspired by heroic courage, unsheath their swords, and on their knees implore heaven's aid in the impending struggle, in a

VOCAL APPEAL TO THE THRONE OF GRACE.

Men, on the square.

Almighty Father, throned on high,
To vict'ry be our guide.
Oh, hear us when to Thee we cry,
In Thy strength we confide.

Women, in church.

Oh, Blessed Virgin, 'tis through thee
We reach the mercy seat,
Before thee, lo, we bow the knee,
And worship at thy feet.
Hear, holy mother, hear.

Combined Chorus.

Oh, heavenly Father, mercy shew,
And help us in our need.
Strengthen our arms in battle's blow.
That Venice may be freed.

Uomini (sulla piazza).

Possente Iddio ci guida
Alla vittoria ancor.
Un popolo confida
Nel Tuo potere ognor.

Donne (nel tempio).

Salga o madre del ciel
La nostra prece a te.
Qui si prostra al tuo piè
Il Popolo fedel.
Salve o madre del ciel

Tutti—(Sulla piazza e in chiesa).

Signor a noi sorrida
La santa tua pietà;
Signor! Tu ancor ci guida
Al sol di libertà.

Contarini now appears with his sword in his right hand, holding aloft the banner of San Marco in his left. Though old in years, he is young in heart and courage. He then vows never to return alive except as a victor, and amid martial music and the blare of trumpets preparations are made for the departure of the Doge, Pisani, the Senate, and the nobles, on the barges which are to bear them to the fleet, which is anchored in the waters of the Lido, near Venice. Gondolas filled with ladies and children, the wives and families of Venetian soldiers who are about to embark, flit around the war barges, while other boats, filled with maidens whose smiling faces conceal sad hearts, as they bid a fond good-bye to those to whom they have pledged eternal love.

The marine cortege is now formed, and Doge Contarini encased in glittering armour, with a helmet on his head, amid the fanfare of trumpets, the ringing of bells, and the shouts of his people, together with Pisani and followers embark on the Ducal barge. As it leaves the quay, the Doge, standing erect as a pine tree, grasps the flag of San Marco, his sword is sheathed and a determined smile of heroism illumines his face. All who are able to fight are ready to go on aboard, and the great naval procession moves slowly away amid

MARTIAL SONGS AND INSPIRING MUSIC.

Hail to the Doge, may vict'ry on him shine!
Hail to thee, Prince, may fortune good be thine.
Our leader great, he is our champion bold,
His prowess long in story will be told.
Not only chief, he is our father kind.
All hail, oh, warlike chief.

Tutti.

Salve al Doge; a lui vittoria,
A te sia laude o nostro principe
Sia laude a te
Campione e duce; sei tu dell' Adria
Il padre e il Re.
Salve al Doge nostra gloria.

END OF ACT I.

ACT II.

Scene I.

THE FORTRESS OF CHIOGGIA.

Here is disclosed a bivouac of the Genoese soldiers and sailors, now, as they fondly imagine, freed from further warfare for a while. They are endeavouring to pass away their spare time by gaming, chatting, and lounging about. Not having any active duties on hand, they indulge in a

MILITARY DANCE,

which is scarcely ended when, in the far distance, the Venetian Fleet is seen approaching, and the Genoese are, for a time, in the utmost confusion. Hurried preparations are made to meet the coming attack, and the men are soon at their posts in battle array.

An attack is made by the Venetian Fleet on Chioggia, but the Genoese, fighting bravely under the command of their intrepid officers, succeed in repelling it. The Venetians, discomfited, but not discouraged, are seen to retreat.

The Genoese, flushed with victory, although exhausted with the heat and toil of battle, celebrate their successful defence in a true soldier-like fashion. They have been closely besieged by the Venetians in the City and Fortress of Chioggia for some time, and hunger, and even thirst, has been pressing them. Some of the soldiers, having made a foray, had captured an ox and some sheep, and these they speedily prepare to cook, together with a supply of vegetables brought by the village girls.

Fruit has also been brought by the villagers, who join the soldiers in their gaiety. Despite the privations they have suffered, they are gay and jovial, and when a cask of wine is found in a hitherto unsuspected hiding place by some of the men, their spirits burst forth in

BACCHANALIAN SONG,

Come, empty the cup! For strength is in wine, and courage 'twill bring. The goblet fill up, With juice of the vine, we laugh, dance and sing. Hark! the drum, rataplan! rataplan! So let the toast pass, and empty your glass, Rataplan! rataplan!	Beviam, beviamo; Nel vin cerchiamo forza e valor Coll' alma in festa Viva si desta la gioja in cor. Ed ora rantaplan—battiamo plan, plan Lieti o fratelli, beviam, beviam E . . . . rantaplan, plan, plan. . . .
Replenish the flask! To Bacchus we'll yield, but ne'er in the fight. Let's empty the cask; We'll die in the field, but drink until light. Hark! the drum, rataplan! rataplan! Etc., etc.	Beviam, godiamo. Se nelle lotte—noi morirem Vuotiamo la botte Che tutta notte—lieti sarem Ed ora il rantaplan, ecc., ecc.
With beauty and wine No man can repine; They make our heads turn, they make our hearts burn. Huzza for the strife and pleasures of life. Hark! the drum, etc., etc.	Donnine belle Coll' alma in festa Gira la testa—ci batte il cor Viva la guerra E l'allegria Giuoco e follia—donne ed amor Ed ora il rantaplan—battiam, ecc.

in which they are joined by their fair companions, accompanied by the martial roll of drums.

This unaccustomed merriment is rudely interrupted by the arrival of *Zeno's* fleet in the offing, and, strengthened by this reinforcement, which has been long and eagerly looked for, the Venetians once more advance to the attack. A terrific onslaught now ensues, in which the Venetians, struggling as they are for home

THE VICTORY AT CHIOGGIA

and liberty, fight with the energy of despair, and gain a complete victory.

Despite the gallant resistance of the besieged army, the hurling of huge stones, the rain of hot pitch by Greek and Dalmatian mercenaries, and the determined stand made at every point by the Genoese, the Venetians succeed in placing their scaling ladders. By impetuous charges they effect the storming of Chioggia amid a wild and fierce scene of hand to hand fighting, in which the flower of Venetian nobility, clad in complete steel, lead the way. The warriors rush over all obstructions, and, amidst the deafening shouts of the elated Venetians, the banner of St. Mark replaces the Genoese flag on the ramparts; and the Doge Contarini, despite his great age, Admiral Pisani, General Zeno, and all the chiefs, assemble on the battlements of the fortress they have so gallantly won.

SCENE II.

AN ISLAND NEAR VENICE.

News of the great victory, and the fall of Chioggia, having been received at Venice, great preparations are made to receive the victors in a manner befitting their feats of arms. Pending their arrival, the day is devoted to

NATIONAL REJOICINGS & AMUSEMENTS.

All kinds of sports are indulged in, including the ever popular Aquatic Tournament by the senior apprentices of rival Glass Manufacturers, the victors in which receive their reward as much in the glances of approbation from the eyes of their fair friends as from the more tangible spoils of victory.

The approach of the

GRAND AQUATIC VICTORY PROCESSION

is now heralded, and a welcome of extraordinary enthusiasm is accorded to the triumphant conquerors by the beauty of Venice.

After the approach of the gay festival gondolas of the nobility, the ceremonial barges representing the

FOUR SEASONS

Winter, Spring, Summer and Autumn, appear, the occupants of which, in symbolic attire, sing a tuneful ode to the seasons.

Male Chorus on the Barge of Winter.

In low and mournful accents,
Does the forest sing its song—
This is the saddest season ;
Ah, the golden days are gone.
The trees were gay and happy,
Now the snow has dressed them white.
And earth's soft velvet cov'ring
Is hidden from our sight.
And tears of ice the branches weep,
Nature is wrapped in slumber deep.

Mormora la foresta
La sua cupa canzon ;
Compagne, è questa, è questa
La più triste stagion.
Alberi un giorno arditi
Or vi copre la neve
Col suo lenzuolo bianco
Di gelo il manto greve
Vi ha resi intirizziti . . .
E il cuore è triste e stanco.

Female Chorus on the Barge of Spring.

Sweetly does the throstle sing,
Heralding the gentle spring.
Buds of April now are seen,
Bursting forth in tender green.
Gaily now the meadows bloom,
Joyous after winter's gloom ;
And the dawn, the birds, the flowers,
All are brightened by love's powers.

Canta la capinera :
Giunge la primavera.
Spunta col dolce april
Il fiorellin gentil.
Vago verdeggia il prato,
Palpita il cor beato ;
L'augello, l'aura, il fior
Han fremiti d'amor.

Female Chorus on the Barge of Summer.

See, the fruitful valley heaves,
Glitt'ring in a sea of sheaves ;
From the mighty mountain's brow
Calmness spreads to plains below.
The blazing sun at noontide smiles,
The ocean calmly sleeps.

Già per le valli apriche
Dardeggia in mar di spiche
La calma alta sorride
Su dalla vètta al pian.
Il sol gagliardo ride . . .
E dorme l'ocean.

Male Chorus on the Barge of Autumn.

The golden fruit of the vine	Coi bei grappoli d'ôro
In garlands we will entwine;	Nor ci intrecciamo il criñ.
To heaven our hymn will rise,	S'alza per l'etra un coro
Praise God, Almighty and wise.	Al nume alto e divin.
The birds are silent with grief,	Ma tristi son gli augelli,
The trees soon lose their last leaf.	Son mesti gli arboscelli
For now 'twixt earth and sky	Perche d'un grigio vel
A thick grey veil doth lie.	Si copri terra e ciel.

Grand Ensemble.

This world is merely folly,	Il mondo è una follia
And turns as pleasures pass;	Che gira col piacer. . . .
And mirth and melancholy,	Il pianto o l'allegria
Are in the emptied glass.	Sta in fondo del bicchier.

These are followed by barges emblematic of the Adriatic and of the Arts, that and containing the Ambassadors, and the Ecclesiastical Barge.

Female Chorus on Barge of "The Arts."

Glory shall follow us along,	La gloria ci accompagna
A golden prize.	Coi raggi d'or.
But art is like fleeting song,	E l'arte una chimera
That quickly dies.	Che, sorge e muor.

Female Chorus on Barge of "The Adriatic."

Thrice happy sea of azure hue,	O mar giulivo e placido
The sun hath thee embraced.	Azzuro e lieto mar,
The glowing orb greets thee with joy	Ti bacia dolce e vivido
And burning kisses chaste.	Il sol che or lieto appar.

Male Chorus on the Ambassadors' Barge.

We, ambassadors from nations	Noi siam di estrani lidi
Distant far from Venice great,	Guerrieri ambasciator
Feel our hearts and senses dazzled,	Cotanta gloria i fascino
By the splendour of the State.	Ci ammalia sensi e cor.

Male Chorus on the Ecclesiastical Barge.

Oh, protect us mighty Lord,	Ci guida tu Signore,
Watch o'er us all our days.	Deh! Ci proteggi Tu,
We, inspired by love divine,	E noi con santo amore
Will ever sing thy praise.	Cantiam le tue virtù.

Grand Ensemble.

This world is merely folly,	Il mondo è una follia
And turns as pleasures pass.	Che gira col piacer
And mirth and melancholy	Il pianto o l'allegria
Are in the emptied glass.	Sta in fondo del bicchier.

The State Barge of Venice,

"THE BUCENTAUR,"

now appears, bearing the grey-headed Doge, surrounded by his warrior chiefs, nobles and others. At the conclusion of this grand pageant, the Doge, standing in the prow of the superb barge, performs the annual ceremony of

THE MARRIAGE OF THE ADRIATIC,

when the assembled concourse of people break forth into song.

Bride of the sea, so mighty is thy power,
Too great to be contained by land.
Thy prowess spread to foreign strand ;
Thy fame and glory increase hour by hour.

Beneath thy mighty standard here unfurled,
Queen of the Adriatic sea,
Thy children ever shall be free,
And tell thy glory to the wondering world.

Sposa al Mar la tua forza e il tuo poter
E a l'azzurro infinito
Alza il vessillo ardito
Ch'è simbolo di gloria e di Saper.

Salve, Salve o Venezia, o tu regina
Dell' Adriaco mar,
A te Salve o divina
La tua gloria nessun potrà offuscar.

This grand and impressive ceremony concluded, and the Doge having retired, the populace continue their amusements, and now Venice is seen in her brightest, and in a joyous holiday mood. The people abandon themselves entirely to enjoyment, and a

VENETIAN REGATTA

takes place, with realistic gondola races, etc., etc.

THE RETURN OF THE VICTORS.

Scene III.

TERRACE OF PORTIA'S PALACE.

The scene discloses a

GRAND BANQUET

given by Portia to the conquering heroes on the terrace of her Palace. In rich and gorgeous robes, and glittering with rare jewels, are the Doge Contarini, and the chief nobles of Venice. Bassanio and Gratiano are once more by the side of those they love, and the universal happiness is musically rendered by a

FESTIVE CHORUS.

Brindisi.

	Tutti 1.
See, the foaming, sparkling wine,	Gùi vivido spumeggia
In the bowl it bubbles.	E circolando ondeggia
Golden essence, thou'rt divine,	Entro il bicchiere
Wine drowns all our troubles.	Color dell' ambra e l'or
Ah, golden wine.	L'almo licor.
Raise we now a song of pleasure,	Inneggiassi all' amore
While of love we think.	Ed al piacere
Love, ah, love, our heart's chief treasure.	Che parlano al mia core
Quickly—let us drink.	Presto, da bere . . .
	2.
Wine to us the path will show	Col vin s'apre la via
Where love lies mid laughter,	Al riso e alla follia,
In the cup the bubbles glow,	Entro il bicchiere
Pleasures follow after.	Color dell'ambra e l'or
Ah, golden wine.	Danza il licor
Thus we sing of joy and gladness	Sia gloria al biondo amore
Pleasure without pain.	Ed al piacere
How with love we'll banish sadness,	Che parlano al mio core;
And—the cup we'll drain.	Versa da bere.

While the guests are thus expressing their happiness, Portia and Nerissa have been asking their lovers the reason why the rings they have vowed so solemnly to keep were not on their fingers. Their assertions that this was the only recompense that would be accepted by the Advocate who rescued Antonio from his perilous position, and his clerk, are received with incredulity, but the promise breaking lovers are forgiven.

The Venetians, in the exultation and enthusiasm of the victory, have generously freed their Genoese prisoners, and these are seen wending their weary way back to their native city. Their dejected appearance touches the noble heart of Portia, and she stops the rejoicings for a time to minister to the more pressing needs of the travellers, whom she asks to remain during the remainder of the festivities, and on whom she bestows rich gifts, in which she is joined by her friends.

After this episode the gaieties are resumed, and a

GRAND FESTAL DANCE,

specially prepared by Portia as the crowning piece of her entertainment, is performed by the maidens of the Venetian Isles.

Here is portrayed the mimic storming and capture of the

CASTLE OF LOVE,

and the triumph in succession of

MORNING, NOON, EVENING AND NIGHT,

terminating in a grand

BALABILE VENEZIANO,

after the conclusion of which, to the infinite surprise of all present, the young and successful Doctor of Laws and his clerk appear, and to the great astonishment, and not less to the joy of all, Portia and Nerissa are recognised on the disguising habilaments being thrown aside.

The fête is concluded by a

GRAND VENETIAN AL FRESCO CARNIVAL,

concluding with a grand national chorus

Venice, dear city, hail!
May victories great
Be showered by fate
And fall on thee.
May thy fame never pale
See, people and king,
As tribute they bring.
All bow the knee.

Salve a te, o patria;
Nova vittoria
Più viva gloria
Fulge su te.
Salve dell' Adria
Fata e regina
A te s'inchina
Popolo e re.

MODERN VENICE

Exhibits a perfect representation of the choicest portions of this unique city as it is to-day. Each building is a solid *fac-simile* of some one world-renowned Palazzo of the Queen City of the Adriatic. The famous RIALTO BRIDGE, with its shops on either side, forming a delightful Children's Paradise.

GONDOLAS, propelled by native Gondoliers, are at the disposal of the visitors. Two landing-stages are provided, one near the Addison Road entrance, and the other near the entrance to Modern Venice. For the small charge of Sixpence per person, a trip through all the ways of Venice may be enjoyed, landing near the Rialto Bridge, close to the Café Rialto. If Modern Venice be entered on foot, the return trip, of an equal distance, may be taken. Special Venetian officials are stationed on the different streets and places to guide the public, and to give such information as may be desired.

THE FINE ART GALLERY, situated on the upper floor, at the East end of the Building, contains a superb collection of Pictures and Sculpture, by the leading artists of Italy, including some choice specimens from the easel of the late Sig. Favretto, a young Venetian artist, recently deceased, whose works are already very difficult to obtain and rarely met with outside his native land.

THE EXHIBITS are shown by the leading manufacturers of Venice, and include fine examples of the various Arts and Crafts for which the Venetians are so deservedly famous, including Hammered Iron, Mosaic Work, Glass, Toys, Filigree Work in Silver, High-class Jewellery, &c., &c.

THE CAFÉ RIALTO, at the foot of the Rialto Bridge, will supply the visitor with the choicest Italian dainties, wines, etc., and tables and chairs are placed on the terrace, close down to the water's edge.

VENETIAN GLASS WORKS. A special and important Annex has been erected by DR. SALVIATI for the purpose of shewing in course of production, his world-renowned Art-work in Venetian Glass, to this Exhibit a charge of 6d., will be made by him.

THE PEAL OF BELLS. By Messrs. HARRINGTON, LATHOM & Co., of Coventry, manufacturers of Harrington's Patent Tubular Bells.

REFRESHMENTS.—The greatest possible care has been, and will be exercised in this department, so that visitors may rely upon obtaining really good refreshments at moderate charges.

THE ARUNDEL SOCIETY'S EXHIBITS.

The exhibits of the Arundel Society include some of the best of the Water Colour copies of Frescoes, Monuments and other artistic treasures in Italy, which have been made for the Council by thoroughly trained Artists, working under careful supervision. It is remarkable that the work of this Society, which has for more than forty years been rescuing from oblivion some of the most important works of the Early Italian School, notably those that are neglected, or are in out of the way localities, should be so little known to the general public, but for the advantages it offers to those becoming members, by the return in the form of reproductions, are so great that Annual Subscribers receive more than the value of their Subscriptions in admirable copies of early Italian works of Art, and at the same time they are justified in thinking that they are materially helping in the work of preserving records of works of Art which are often inaccessable, and, unfortunately, even more often suffering from the neglect or ignorance of their custodians.

It is of course indisputable that Frescoes and Mural Paintings generally are specially exposed to injury, and unlike panel pictures, and other portable works of Art, can, with rare exceptions, only be studied on the spot. It has been the endeavour therefore of the Council of the Arundel Society to bring these before the public by means of Chromo-lithography, it having been found possible, by the employment of the most elaborate form of this process, to obtain almost absolute fac-similes of the Water-colour Copies which, as mentioned above, are made on the spot by the highly trained Artists. When it is added that on the Council of the Society may be found, among others, the names of Sir A. H. Layard, G.C.B., Sir William Gregory, K.C.M.G., Lord Carlisle (all trustees of the National Gallery), Sir Frederick Burton (Director of the National Gallery), and E. J. Poynter, R.A., it will be seen that the affairs of the Society are sure to be administered with due regard to the Artistic value of the subjects which may be copied or which may be reproduced by Chromo-lithography.

The offices of the Society are at 19, St. James' Street, S.W.; and full information as to membership, &c., can be obtained there from the Secretary, Douglas H. Gordon, Esq., or from the attendant in charge of the Society's exhibit in "Venice in London."

THE PAINTED GLASS IN THE HALL OF THE DOGE'S RESTAURANT

Consists of a number of Historical, Mythological, and Allegorical Figures. Over the principal entrances occur four of the Doges in full ducal costume. On either side are the figures of Homer, Cervantes, Chaucer, Dante, Milton and Shakespeare. On the opposite side are figures of the Greek Mythology, viz., Jupiter and Juno, Venus and Minerva, Paris and Helen, Proserpine and Pluto, Apollo and Diana. The Allegorical Figures represent Music, Painting, Sculpture and Science.

The lower windows contain a representation of the Lion of St. Mark's. The glass is for sale as a whole, or in separate panels, or replicas can be had, the cost of which can be ascertained at the Office.

The Glass is designed and executed in the highest type of glass painting; and it has been specially painted for the "Hall of the Doges," and is the work of the well-known artist, Mr. EDWARD FRAMPTON, 110, Buckingham Palace Road, S.W., the designer of many important works.

The window in the building across the canal, facing the Rialto, is also lent by the same artist; and another window illustrating *Jacob's Dream*.

DOULTON & CO.,

Lambeth Sanitary Engineering Works,

LAMBETH, LONDON, S.E.

PATENT "SIMPLICITAS" CLOSET.

THE CLOSET—SLOP-SINK—AND URINAL.

This Closet is constructed in one piece of STONEWARE, or QUEENSWARE.

The **Stoneware**, by reason of its great strength, is specially adapted for use in buildings where it is liable to rough usage.

The **Queensware**, is of highly-finished quality and appearance, and may be had White or with Surface Ornamentation, and is suitable for the best class of work.

This Closet is specially constructed to work with a syphon cistern.

By its peculiar formation all parts are thoroughly cleansed at each flush.

The back is so formed that the soil must fall into the water of the trap, and the flushing rim is reduced to a minimum, in order to prevent its being fouled in use where it cannot be flushed.

It is compact and neat in appearance.

The whole of the Sanitary Appliances in the Retiring Rooms in this building have been supplied and fixed by us, where they may be seen in action,

ALSO AT

Lambeth & 75a, Queen Victoria St., E.C.

PAISLEY & PARIS.

The Times says:—"The 'Church Monthly' is excellent."

24 Pages Crown 4to, & 32 Pages Demy 8vo.

PRICE ONE PENNY,

THE CHURCH MONTHLY,

Edited by FREDK. SHERLOCK,

Author of "More than Conquerors," &c.

Late Hon. Editorial Secretary of the Church of England Temperance Society.

The Church Monthly is admitted by the Bishops, Clergy, and Press alike to be conspicuous among Parish Magazines for the High Artistic Character of its Illustrations, the excellence of its Literary Contributions, and the varied interest of its Contents.

The Church Monthly is conducted entirely on non-party lines, so that any Clergyman adopting it may rest assured that the Magazine will never introduce a partisan spirit among his parishioners.

The Church Monthly is LOCALISED in every Diocese in England and Wales, and is largely circulated in the Colonies and on the Continent.

The Church Monthly inserts no Appeals for Funds under any circumstances, so that the Clergy never find their Appeals in the Local Pages rivalled by Appeals for Societies or purely London objects in the body of the Magazine.

The Bookseller says:—"'THE CHURCH MONTHLY.' The success which has attended the career of this excellent Magazine has been so extraordinary as to show that the efforts of its proprietary to produce—at a liberal expenditure of money—a thoroughly high-class periodical suitable for localisation have been duly appreciated. It is not too much to say that no other magazine of the kind can compare with it, either for high standard of literary merit, breadth and clearness of view, or excellence of production. The bound volume for the year is before us, and makes an exceedingly readable and handsome volume.

The Church Monthly is the Largest and most profusely Illustrated Penny Magazine ever published.

SPECIMEN COPIES, with Terms for Localisation, will be sent post free to any address, on application to Mr. FREDK. SHERLOCK, 30 *and* 31, *New Bridge Street, Ludgate Circus, E.C.*

The Yorkshire Post says:—"The 'Church Monthly' proves itself to be the BEST Magazine for Parish Localisation."

In Royal 4to. Artistic Picture Cover. Price 1s.

THE ONLY AUTHORISED BOOK FOR CHILDREN ON

VENICE IN LONDON:

IMRE KIRALFY'S

WONDERLAND FOR CHILDREN.

The most charming Toy Book ever produced. Full of magnificent Coloured Illustrations of the grand scenes at OLYMPIA, including the Carnival, Venice at Night, Aquatic Scenes, &c. From specially-executed designs by the wellknown-artist, ALFRED JOHNSON.

With a Preface to the Little Ones, by IMRE KIRALFY.

In small Crown 4to. Cloth Gilt. Bevelled Boards. Price 7/6.

"The handsomest Book of the year."—STANDARD.

AN OCEAN KNIGHT:

A Story of the Corsairs and their Conquerors.

Translated from the French of FORTUNÉ DU BOISGOBEY. Fully Illustrated with upwards of Sixty Artistic Engravings from designs by ADRIEN MARIE.

This Volume contains many effective incidents of Venetian Life, Illustrations of the celebrated Carnival, and full descriptions of the well-known wars on the Mediterranean.

NUTTALL'S

100,000 REFERENCES.

3/6 STANDARD PRONOUNCING 3/6

THREE HUNDRED AND FIFTEENTH THOUSAND.

DICTIONARY.

N.B.—This Edition (1892) is thoroughly revised up to Date.

AN ILLUSTRATED CATALOGUE,

Containing over 3,000 volumes for Presentation, School Prizes, and Children's Books, including fine Editions of the Poets, Standard Literature, Dictionaries, Novels, Practical Handbooks, &c., will be forwarded, post free, on application to

FREDERICK WARNE & CO., Bedford St., Strand, London.

THE STRAND MAGAZINE,

Reduced Fac-simile.

THE

Strand Magazine

is the most interesting, the best illustrated, and the most widely-circulated Sixpenny Magazine in the world.

Started only a year ago, its success has been phenomenal. Of No. 1 more than 375,000 copies have been sold, while the ordinary monthly sales reach a total never before attained in publications of this class.

At least HALF-A-MILLION copies of the Dec. (Christmas) issue will be printed.

THE

STRAND MAGAZINE

PRICE SIXPENCE.

Is issued regularly in the early part of each month.

The **ILLUSTRATIONS** in the STRAND MAGAZINE are by the most eminent Artists, and have been declared by the Press to surpass anything previously offered to the British Public.

The **ARTICLES** and **STORIES** in the STRAND MAGAZINE—profusely illustrated—are by the best literary Authors. The fiction is bright, interesting and wholesome, while the Articles are full of information, conveyed in a crisp entertaining style, which is always readable and never dull.

The STRAND MAGAZINE contains special translations from the first foreign Authors.

VOLUMES ONE & TWO OF THE STRAND MAGAZINE

Beautifully bound in Cloth, with Gilt Edges, containing 1,670 Illustrations,

ARE NOW READY. Price, 6/- each; Post Free, 7½d. each extra.

Binding Covers may be had at 1/- each, postage 3*d*. extra.

7th Thousand.

WHAT'S BRED IN THE BONE.

By GRANT ALLEN. **£1,000** Prize Novel. Price 3/6; Post Free, 3/9.

GEORGE NEWNES, Ltd.,

8, 9, 10 & 11, SOUTHAMPTON STREET, AND EXETER STREET, STRAND, LONDON.

HOW TO REACH "OLYMPIA."

TRAVEL BY THE

DISTRICT RAILWAY.

MOST DIRECT, BEST AND QUICKEST ROUTE

FROM

NEW CROSS, AND ALL EAST LONDON STATIONS,
WHITECHAPEL, ALDGATE EAST,
MARK LANE, MONUMENT, CANNON ST.,
ALSO FROM
HOUNSLOW, OSTERLEY,
EALING, ACTON,
RICHMOND, KEW GARDENS,
CHISWICK PARK, TURNHAM GREEN, &c.

BOOK TO **WEST KENSINGTON.**

AND FROM

MANSION HOUSE (CENTRAL CITY STATION),
BLACKFRIARS, TEMPLE,
CHARING CROSS,
WESTMINSTER, ST. JAMES' PARK,
VICTORIA,
SLOANE SQUARE, SOUTH KENSINGTON,
EARLS COURT, &c., &c.,
WALHAM GREEN, PUTNEY, SOUTHFIELDS,
WIMBLEDON.

BOOK TO **ADDISON ROAD** OR **WEST KENSINGTON.**

10 TRAINS HOURLY FROM MANSION HOUSE, &c.

FREQUENT TRAINS FROM ALL OTHER STATIONS.

EXTRA LATE TRAINS AS REQUIRED.

COLLINS & WESTOBY,

TAILORS,

40, WEST STRAND,

LONDON, W.

NAVAL, MILITARY AND COURT UNIFORMS.

LADIES' HABITS, WALKING COSTUMES.

ARE NOW SHOWING SPECIALITIES IN

LLAMA, VICUNAS, AND SHETLAND WOOL GOODS for Gentlemen's Suits at 50/-.

ANGOLA, SCOTCH TWEED and CASHMERE TROUSERS, 13/-

Boys' Eton Suits, to Order, 42/-
And Evening Dress Suits, lined Silk, 70/-

Indian and Colonial Outfits made at 48 hours notice.

N.B.—*We are the makers of the Venetian Uniform worn by the Ushers at "Venice in London."*

PATENT ROLL SCREENS.

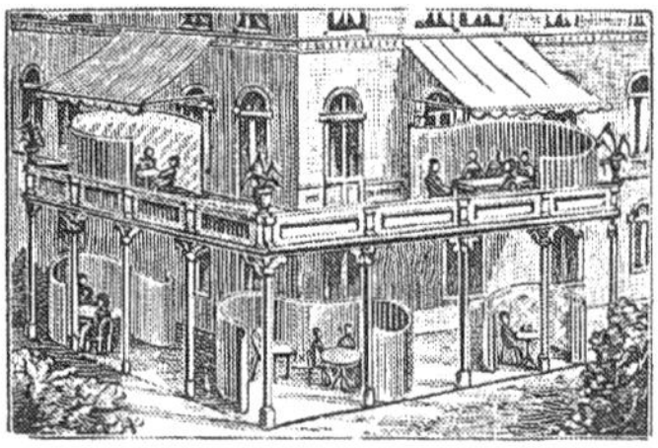

To be obtained from Furniture Dealers.

OR

WHOLESALE ONLY.

FROM

E. & O. QUITMANN, 18, City Road, Finsbury Square, London.

Riddle & Couchman, Printers, 22, Southwark Bridge Road, London.

Pears' soap.
BY ROYAL
APPOINTMENT
SOAP MAKERS
To Her Majesty
THE QUEE
The Purest
best for the Skin
and most economical
in use.
PEARS.
SOAPMAKERS BY SEALED APPOINTMENT
To H.R.H. The PRINCE of WAL

Milton Keynes UK
Ingram Content Group UK Ltd.
UKHW020626291024
2435UKWH00004B/47

9 781020 517532